OPEN ROAD

*The Adventure of a Breakthrough
Prayer Initiative*

Sue Nilson Kibbey

the greatest
EXPEDITION

OPEN ROAD

The Adventure of a Breakthrough Prayer Initiative

©2021 Sue Nilson Kibbey

books@marketsquarebooks.com
P.O. Box 23664   Knoxville, Tennessee 37933
ISBN: 978-1-950899-21-0
Library of Congress: 2021931621

Printed and Bound in the United States of America
Cover Illustration & Book Design ©2021 Market Square Publishing, LLC
Publisher: Kevin Slimp
Editors: Kristin Lighter and Kay Kotan
Post-Process Editor: Ken Rochelle

This resource was commissioned as
one of many interconnected steps in the
journey of *The Greatest Expedition.*

the greatest
EXPEDITION

GreatestExpedition.com

I'm grateful...

for my father, Richard Wayne Livingston,
  who has always instilled in me courage to pursue
  the open road of life's untraversed possibilities

And for Gavin Ray and Beckett Wayne,
  young next-generation world changers for Christ
  whose growing open road eagerness
    inspires me, ongoing,
      with expectation for all God has in store up ahead.

Table of Contents

Foreword 1
by Kay Kotan

Intro 3
Start Here

Chapter 1 7
Church of the Open Road

Chapter 2 23
Open Road: Removing Roadblocks

Prayer Roadblocks Removal Guide 43

Chapter 3 49
Breakthrough Prayer Initiative Wayfinder

Breakthrough Prayer Initiative 79
A Guide to Help You with Implementation

Chapter 4 83
Open Road Survival Equipment: Specialty
Breakthrough Practices

FOREWORD

By Kay Kotan

This resource was commissioned as one of many interconnected steps in the journey of *The Greatest Expedition*. While each step is important individually, we intentionally built the multi-step Essentials Pack and the Expansion Pack to provide a richer and fuller experience with the greatest potential for transformation and introducing more people to a relationship with Jesus Christ. For more information visit **GreatestExpedition.org**.

However, we also recognize you may be exploring this resource apart from *The Greatest Expedition.* You might find yourself on a personal journey, a small group journey, or perhaps a church leadership team journey. We are so glad you are on this journey!

As you take this first step and subsequent steps into your expedition, your Expedition Team

1

will discover whether all the ministry tools you will be exploring will be utilized only for the Expedition Team or if this expedition will be a congregational journey. **Please note:** Whenever the leadership team is referenced in this resource, it is synonymous with the Expedition Team for a solo expedition.

Regardless of how you came to discover the *Open Road*, it will pave the way to a new God-inspired expedition. It is with great intentionality that this resource is the first ministry tool offered to you, the Expedition Team, as you prepare for the expedition God is calling you into. As you implement by using the guidance and examples provided, expect to see breakthroughs begin to unfold. Then as you continue to explore and deploy subsequent ministry tools in The Greatest Expedition series, you'll already have established a vital practice of breakthrough prayer that will continue to grow and spread. Prayer is the first step before setting out on the "open road" of your expedition–wherever this journey may take you.

Kay L Kotan, PCC
Director, *The Greatest Expedition*

INTRODUCTION

Church of the Open Road

It is my joy to share with you through the following pages what has become an awe-and-amazement-filled calling.

I "cannot stop speaking what I've seen and heard," to use the phrase the early disciples coined (Acts 4:20) as they witnessed the initial movement of Jesus called the Church, surging forward and outward.

The church of Jesus, you see, was never meant to be merely a group of goodhearted, inwardly focused religious people, collective energy invested in caring for one another, ensuring adequate building upkeep for in-person activities, and managing finances to keep everything afloat.

Instead, the distinguishing hallmark of the movement of Christ followers called the Church is to be an expectant focus *up and out* in pursuit of uncharted spiritual adventure to embrace and transform the world. Read the entire book of Acts in the Bible's New Testament, and then read it carefully again. It's the original dynamic illustration of what God still intends.

So, if that's the Divine hope for every church, I'll ask a question some of you may have already wondered yourselves.

What's gone wrong in a perfectly good faith-filled, well-intentioned, settled-in congregation that's instead become plateaued or even started into decline? Maybe like yours, or a church that you know?

Perhaps it's happened gradually as the church has become comfortable and complacent over time. Or, maybe the rapidly changing factors of our current community and world environment have resulted in us church-goers hanging on even more tightly to each other, our facility and our budget to just survive?

"What's gone wrong?" we wonder. A better question might be to ask, *What is missing?* The answer to that question is straightforward and non-negotiable. And it's my desire to help you embrace and deploy the missing ingredient anew in your own personal life, your expedition, and in the life of your church.

You, too, can set the stage for shifting a stagnant congregational campout circled around a comfortable, predictable campfire together to instead responding to the Divine prompting to the open road. With this added ingredient you, too, can expect to see your church advance according to the Almighty's bidding forward.

But first, maybe we've met before ? Or perhaps this book is our first ministry training together. And if so, glad to meet you.

I'm a church pastor, trainer, consultant and author who has been following the Holy Spirit's relentless leading to every part of our country. As a ministry practitioner I've been sharing with countless numbers of churches, leaders and members a set of simple, practical steps to guide their addition of this mainspring missing ingredient to church life and leadership. What I have witnessed unfolding is a growing movement of miraculous new spiritual vitality beyond what I could have ever imagined!

As the amazing stories from church after church keep rolling in, I have also become a storyteller.

I'm unable to resist recounting the breakthroughs at churches large, small, rural, suburban, urban, historic, new, multiethnic, multicultural—all bearing witness to the endlessly creative ways God has invited them onward to actively deliver and fulfill the message and mission of Christ.

Bottom line, my intent is to ensure that our companionship through the pages of this small book inspire you about what is Divinely possible, provide you a practical path of steps you can take with ideas you could deploy to add this ingredient and recount a few of the many stories from your sister churches (names have been changed) that may add to your inspiration.

Everything is with the heartfelt hope that you, too, can set the stage for your own and your church's next future chapter, and to enable you to recognize God's irresistible summons to the open road—which is that greatest expedition of all.

CHAPTER ONE

Church of the Open Road

Do you remember Walt Whitman's classic poem about the "open road?" Here are a few favorite lines.

Maybe you, like me, can almost feel the fresh, inviting breeze of a beautiful new morning caressing your face as you read the following.

Afoot and light-hearted, I take to the open road,
Healthy, free, the world before me,
The long brown path before me, leading
wherever I choose.

. . . From this hour, freedom!
From this hour I ordain myself loos'd of limits and
imaginary lines.

. . . I inhale great draughts of space;
The east and the west are mine, and the north and
the south are mine.

I will recruit for myself and you as I go;
I will scatter myself among men and women as I go;
I will toss the new gladness and roughness
among them;

Whoever denies me, it shall not trouble me;
Whoever accepts me, he or she shall be blessed, and
shall bless me.

If you're not completely familiar with the term "open road," try this definition: a beckoning to set out upon an unknown, irresistible new journey instead of taking the usual routine route.

The open road typically offers less traffic, fewer stoplights. You can likely travel for a long time without reaching anything familiar, if ever. Along with inhaling "great draughts of space" and marveling at invigorating new scenery, however, you may well encounter rough or unpaved roads, unexpected weather, and increasing distance away from familiar remedies when challenges arise. You may be forced to improvise or real-time troubleshoot. Even so, open road foot travelers on an unaccustomed path also celebrate what's been nicknamed "trail magic." That's when along the way, out of nowhere, appear unexpected resources, needed guidance or morale-boosting blessings. And there are even sometimes "trail angels," individuals who materialize out of seemingly thin air to offer a helping hand at just the right moment.

Oh, the intoxicating, daring, insurgent

summons—and the bold freedom of saying yes to the open road!

The spiritual journey following Jesus, from the start, has been just such a daring invitation, a summons to the open road. When Jesus began his active earthly ministry, he walked beside the lakefront and invited individuals to join him. Take a look in the book of Matthew (chapter 3) for an account of how Jesus asked fishermen brothers Peter and Andrew to come along. Then another pair of fishermen, James and John, also said yes to his invite. They plus others, at times many others, together followed Jesus daily on the open road for the next few years as they learned from, ministered alongside and eventually stepped out of their comfort zones with him. Something fueled their growing risk-it-all, wide-eyed confidence in the One they followed. They eventually became transformed into faith-filled leaders who ended up literally changing the world by delivering the hope, love and Good News everywhere—with ripples of their world-changer impact right through history to today. Jesus' twelve disciples were the original expeditioners!

Have you ever traveled anywhere with a group of people? If so, you know what a host of differing opinions, perspectives, preferences and suggested solutions end up emerging whenever the unexpected arises. Now, then, can you imagine Jesus and his followers on their *three-year* group walking trip together?

Day in and day out, they encountered occasions that required problem-solving to maximize use of their time, their resources, their responses to individuals and multitudes gathering around and even to find waypoints to which they were headed. Scripture reveals his road companions had no shortage of views and advice to offer their leader Jesus. But time and again, their proposed methodology differed from the tactic of Jesus by a decisive ingredient that Jesus always insisted on incorporating. As you've read the Gospels, have you ever noticed this?

Here are a few examples:

- When it got late after a long day where Jesus had been teaching a large gathering, his roadies proposed a plan to send them away hungry so they could find and buy their own food. Jesus agreed the people needed a plan to get fed, but added his special ingredient. He told his disciples to organize everyone to sit down, then *prayed* over the disciples' own personal small dinner supply of loaves and fish. Afterwards he directed his traveling posse to serve it to all 5,000 people. As they followed Jesus' instructions, the disciples were astounded it had become miraculously more than enough for everyone (Matthew 14:15-21).

- A woman who had been sick for twelve years desperately grabbed at Jesus' cloak as he was jostling through a throng of people, underway to an important appointment. His road traveling group attempted to keep him moving along efficiently, assuring him the touch he'd felt had been no one in particular—only crowds pressing against him. Instead of ignoring the nudge as they had advocated, however, Jesus first stopped. He took time to turn and *speak a simple prayer* of healing that miraculously transformed the woman's life on the spot, then resumed heading to the appointment (Luke 8:43-48).

- After an extended day of ministry when more and more people were still demanding Jesus heal them, the next morning he had instead disappeared. Jesus' traveling companions searched and found where he had gone alone *to pray* and gain spiritual respite. They urged Jesus to return for more overtime ministry work at that location immediately. But Jesus' ministry plan for the day did not include compromising the discernment received in his prayer time. In fact, his prayer-refreshed directive was, "Let's go somewhere else..." (Mark 1:35-37). Rather than stay settled in the same place doing more of the same over again, Jesus led his traveling group back out onto the open road and moving.

- When it became necessary for Jesus to identify his key leaders, he didn't do so by acquiescing to who was the most commanding personality, who might have tried to be the most helpful, who had the most lucrative career background or professional expertise, who had received the best education or who was simply available and might agree out of a sense of duty. Instead, Jesus pulled away by himself and *prayed all night* before intentionally extending individual invitations to become his twelve disciples (Luke 6:14-16).

Jesus' disciples eventually identified the game changer ingredient in his recipe for handling challenges, decisions, timing, relationships and unexpected opportunities. More important than daily nourishing his physical body with food was Jesus' daily (and moment-by-moment) supernatural nourishment of prayer. They witnessed a dramatic resulting contrast between their own self-driven efforts to organize and to minister, and those of Jesus. Jesus' road companions, after two years on the open road with him, finally surrendered their egos, their own human expertise and their mindsets.

And they asked Jesus to teach them to pray. Please understand it was not that they hadn't been praying in various forms throughout their lives already, in whatever ways they'd been taught or learned up till then. But now, they wanted for themselves that miraculous kind of prayer ingredient that Jesus was always adding.

"Lord, teach us to pray..." they pleaded (Luke 11:1).

Jesus did teach them (and us) how to pray. And "the prayer that never fails" as it's been called, the essential ingredient his road companions longed to incorporate as he did, can be found in Matthew 6:10:

This, then, is how you should pray [explained Jesus]:

> *Our Father in heaven,*
> *Hallowed be your name.*
> ***Your kingdom come,***
> ***Your will be done,***
> *On earth as it is in heaven...*

Translators of the original Greek language Jesus spoke have rendered the bolded words into a beautiful English language phrase that most of us know by heart as part of the Lord's Prayer: "Your will **be done**...."

Translated literally, the dynamic Greek verb Jesus utilized usually meant *to come into existence, to break through or emerge in history* or *for miracles to come to pass.* Jesus was teaching his companions (along with asking for forgiveness, daily provision and deliverance from temptation) to add prayer inviting God to also break through current reality with new possibilities!

Jesus' followers grasped that doing ministry and good works via their own human ideas and expertise wasn't enough. When Jesus taught them to add prayer asking God to break through miraculously anew, they began to look expectantly for the Almighty God to do in and through them what they had never imagined on their own and certainly couldn't accomplish themselves. Through the added ingredient of this "breakthrough prayer" practice, as I call it, they became bold partners on the irresistible, uncharted daily summons of the trail-magic-strewn open road following Jesus. Their usual activities of helping, serving and healing became divinely infused. (Read about it in Luke 10:1-24.)

And by the way, on his final evening of earthly open road ministry, Jesus retreated to the Garden of

Gethsemane to spiritually prepare for what would come next. That pivotal night he prayed the same "breakthrough" prayer, with the same Greek verb, he had taught his disciples:

> *[Jesus] went away a second time and prayed, "My Father, if it is not possible for this cup to be taken away unless I drink it, may* **your will be done.**"
>
> **Matthew 26:42**

After Jesus' death, followed by his resurrection, his disciples—his most faithful followers who had walked daily with him—found themselves instead gathered in an upper room supporting one another and wondering what was next (Acts 1). With their beloved leader now physically absent, they had left the road and initially reverted to an inward focus: caring for one another, reorganizing themselves, choosing another leader to replace Judas. And at least they had each other, the hymns they enjoyed singing together, the bread and cup Jesus had encouraged them to keep sharing together, right? They were safe inside, right?

But gathered in that upper room they must have also remembered that just becoming better organized for ministry wasn't enough, as it hadn't been back on the initial journey with Jesus. Sharing together in love and fellowship wasn't enough. Scripture recounts that they re-embraced the mainspring recipe ingredient they had been taught on the open road, and resumed feasting on prayer together—"continually," as the scriptures tell us.

And according to the next chapter of Acts, their prayers received a mighty response. The living and active Spirit of God rallied them right out of the upper room's doors by the siren song of the Divine summons, to again join the now-resurrected Jesus on the open road journey—for always!

The expanding movement of Jesus followers we call the Church still continues across the world today. Its intended identity remains ever a living, vibrant faith journey of the open road, at every step incorporating the prayer ingredient he taught us for the guidance and resources needed underway. This is, indeed, is the Greatest Expedition!

A Defining Question

Now let's pause. Reflect on your own church right now—whether you are a pastor, staff person, leader or member.

Do you view your church as an **organization**, *or a* **movement**?

How you think of your church will determine not only your priorities, but also your energy investment and actions. It will define how you lead and to what extent you live into what the church of Jesus Christ is intended to be.

Look, I've spent years as a church pastor myself. I know it's easiest to migrate towards managing your church as an ongoing set of logistics to be administered and maintained, kept staffed with volunteers to handle duties and financially sustained by the contributions of its members.

Other indications of an **organization mindset** often include these. Are any familiar to you?

- Routinely relying on church leaders' or staff's professional expertise and previous experience as our main source of directional wisdom.

- Using projected limitations of the current bank account balance to automatically restrict new potential ministry opportunities.

- Endlessly discussing and debating our own ideas about what might be humanly possible in our circumstances.

- Urging more church members to step up and help with the plans that leadership has laid out, but seeing little response.

• Listening to the voices of disappointment, discouragement and helplessness both within ourselves and spoken by others regarding our congregation's future.

Now, the other perspective. What might happen if you and your leadership instead began to view and lead your church as a *movement?*

According to one dictionary, a movement can be defined as a "rapid progression of events" or "a series of actions and activities trending towards a new direction." That's quite a different picture from working hard to push a stagnant church forward through organizational maintenance and fine tuning, isn't it?

Indications of a **movement mindset** for church leadership might include:

• Rather than a quick "bookend" prayer to open and end leadership meetings, instead offering a short prayer to set the stage before every agenda item: asking God to open new doors and bring new ideas, to anoint us with new spiritual ears to listen and hear and give us willingness to set aside our own accustomed preferences.

• Instead of a scarcity attitude as we assess our resources, budget or volunteer corps for the future, the leadership team's most urgent and important responsibility shifts from asking each other, "What should we do next?" to asking God what *God* wants to do in and through our church, and through us?

- And with a movement mindset, what if we both modeled ourselves and brought/taught the entire congregation the miraculously motivational ingredient of the kind of prayer Jesus taught us to add, which I call a churchwide *breakthrough prayer initiative?*

You're invited to encounter the discussion/reflection questions at the end of this chapter and explore the evidence you see of organization mindset versus movement mindset in your congregation. Which do you desire, and why?

What's Next

My hope is that you will choose to add an ongoing "Breakthrough Prayer Initiative," which has a simple, remarkable way of proliferating a feast of prayer congregation-wide. But it only takes hold if the church's leaders first model and live it ourselves—and sometimes any of us can hold assumptions about prayer that become roadblocks.

So, in chapter 2 I'd like you to meet a leadership team that might share a few similarities to yours.

You'll observe how they challenged themselves to fundamentally alter and enhance their prayer perspective and prayer assumptions, both individually and together as a team, in order to set the stage for a shift from organization to *movement*.

Lord, teach us to pray...

Discussion/Reflection Questions—Chapter 1

1. Does the concept of the church as an "open road" spiritual adventure excite you, intimidate you, or give you pause? Explain.

2. Would you describe your church right now as:

   • already underway on a "great expedition" or journey following Jesus, actively fulfilling new dimensions of bringing God's love and message to new people right now?

   Or...

   • in a holding pattern as you assess the church's financial and membership viability for the future?

   Or...

- generally resistant to making changes or
  trying much that's new—preferring to enjoy the
  familiarity of traditions, long-time friendships
  and mutual support?

3. Which mindset—*organization* or *movement*—
   would you say best describes your church's
   leadership approach, as well as how the church
   functions? Share examples to support your
   thoughts. Which mindset would you prefer the
   church to have, and why? If it would require
   change, are you open to doing things differently?

4. Would you say your church's general behavior
   reflects/does not reflect a deep conviction that
   prayer makes a difference? What evidence would
   you point to, either way? Is the "evidence" you
   name from your church's past history, or currently?

5. What is happening on a week-to-week basis
   regarding the role and activity of prayer across
   the life of your congregation in your view?
   Make a list of everything that comes to mind.
   On a scale of 1 (little prayer) to 10 (lots of prayer
   involving the majority of the church, all age
   groups), what number on the scale would you
   give your church's active prayer life?

6. How about you personally? On a typical day, or over the course of a week, on a scale where 1 = little/no prayer and 10 = continual prayer, what number would best approximate your own prayer life? Are you satisfied?

Action Step: Personal Prayer Practice

- Choose a schedule for yourself—at least four or more times daily—and set your phone's alarms/timer, or your smart watch alarms, calendar alarms, or make yourself a written note reminder accordingly. Each time, pause and look inward and speak to God, requesting:

"Lord, teach me to pray..."

Then silently continue to pause and listen for at least a minute before moving on with your day's activities. Repeat this simple daily repeated prayer practice for at least a week or longer. Jot down anything that comes to your mind or heart at any point during the "pause and listen" minutes. Be prepared to share at least one note you've made during this prayer practice the next time you meet together with your leadership team, if you are utilizing this book resource together.

CHAPTER TWO

Open Road:
Removing Roadblocks

I remember the moment like it was yesterday. Faith Church's leadership team chairperson Claire had leaned forward, her eyes flashing as she made sure not to mince words while attempting to set me straight.

"What in the world? You are asking us to use our valuable, limited time to discuss our church's *prayer life,* at this specially scheduled future focus work session—with all our key leaders present? And with the urgent financial and declining attendance our church is facing that we must turn around as soon as we can?"

From the facial expressions of all ten leaders in attendance, tension was suddenly invading the atmosphere. "I thought Pastor Milton had explained to you clearly ahead of time that we were inviting you to facilitate us forward in some fresh ways.

We need to nail down a new and different plan the congregation will be willing not only to affirm, but finally this time around also rise up to make happen. So that's what we need from you today. To briefly answer your opening question, of course our church believes prayer is important, and we have a prayer chain and all of that like any church would. But this meeting right now isn't intended to be a Sunday school class on prayer. We leaders are here to get down to business, find action steps to help us keep our church alive and get it moving again. For unknown reasons, we've been stuck."

I had counted it a privilege earlier that fall when Pastor Milton originally contacted me, extending an invitation to attend Faith Church's annual leadership team future focus session. Their task was to outline a strategy forward for the church. If then approved by the entire membership, it would be used as a road map over the coming months for allocation of the church budget and teamwork of all the committees, ideally resulting in evidence of accomplishment and progress by a year later.

"We have excellent thinkers on the leadership team," Pastor Milton had explained beforehand. "A few are local business leaders, like the chairperson

Claire. Others are professionals in our community, a couple are farmers, and we also have different backgrounds and ages from young adult to senior adult long-time members. So, the group overall is knowledgeable about community needs, good financial management and even facility upkeep. We have had a future focus session every year during my ministry at this church, and each time pretty much the same repeat opinions are argued about what could be possible, after which a set of detailed next steps for the church are ultimately defined and agreed upon. But please be aware that the church has never ended up doing much of any of them. The leadership seems to generate enthusiasm and the members are approving when it's all rolled out. We usually highlight every week in our church newsletter the parts of the future focus plans each committee 'should' start working on, but we always end up just continuing to do what we've always done.

"The leadership council is discouraged and grasping at straws. Honestly, I am also at a loss. What are we not doing that we should be doing? What is missing? That's what we'd all like to know."

Back now to the future focus session. "Thank you, Claire. I fully appreciate the immediacy you and everyone feel about your responsibility as Faith Church's leaders. But for the guidance you seek, we must begin with the question I asked. Unless we start there, it's unlikely anything will change for Faith Church. I have a short set of discussion questions I'd like us to consider sequentially, and that's the first one. May I continue?"

Looking around the gathering, I repeated it again.

"Think about the prayer life of your congregation. What role does prayer play, and when?"

"Why, of course we pray here. That's a non-negotiable in any church," Pastor Milton was quick to confirm. "We pray each week during the worship service both live and online: I do a pastoral prayer, and then we all say the Lord's Prayer together. We always open and close meetings with a prayer, including asking about prayer concerns such as who is sick, is suffering hardship or crisis or grief or who needs prayers for protection. We do that at these monthly leadership team meetings without fail—it is always right there on the meeting agenda, so no one forgets. On occasions the congregation gathers for a meal, we always say table grace. And once a year, I try to do a three-week sermon series on prayer when I can fit it in."

"I am the prayer chain chair," added Luciana. "Members call, email or text me regularly with prayer requests because they are or loved ones are undergoing a difficult time, are ill or for other reasons. Faith Church has emailed out a prayer chain list every Monday for years. We even print it in the worship bulletin. It's how everyone keeps up with who is sick, who's had surgery or is hospitalized or something."

We moved on to the second discussion question.

"It sounds like many here would likely affirm they have an intellectual belief that prayer matters. But that's quite different from literally believing that when we pray, it truly does make a difference. As you reflect on it, do you personally believe — really believe — that prayer makes a difference? That when we pray, God responds?"

Most heads nodded, a few vigorously.

"Sure do," spoke up Leland. "Absolutely! I have read stories about how when people have prayed, someone gets miraculously healed. I haven't witnessed it myself, but I am convinced it has and does happen at times. I saw a Youtube video just last week of a person's testimony."

"Well, more often prayer at least helps people become calmer and more focused," Pastor Milton contributed. "I don't think the mechanism of prayer is that we tell God exactly what to do, though, and then expect it to automatically happen just that way as though God is a magical Santa Claus. That's not a biblical definition of prayer. It's certainly not how Jesus talked about it."

Then we moved further.

"Okay, now a third question for you—and give this some thought before you answer. Even if you believe that when we pray—when you pray—it does make a difference, can you think whether you have any 'roadblocks' that, ironically, limit how much or how often you actually do pray?"

Ben looked regretful. "Okay, I'll be the first one to answer that, but it's embarrassing given how many years I've been a Faith Church member attending every week. I'm proud that our church compiles the prayer chain list to make available. I always read through it and find it very informative. But honestly, I have no idea what to specifically pray for each person or situation on that long list. No idea at all. So, I just don't pray for any of them! Maybe it means prayer is not my thing, unfortunately. Hopefully other people like praying through a list, though, and are doing it."

"So, it sounds like for Ben, a prayer roadblock for you is facing a long list you feel you are expected to pray through one by one. Anyone else?"

"Well, I know exactly what mine is," Claire admitted. "I do believe prayer makes a difference, and I have little prayers I pray inside myself when I need to. I guess you could call them 'panic prayers' because they're asking God to help me real quick right then. It could be anything — for the right words to say, or for something I need. I just pray it silently inside, and I know God hears just fine. As everyone has seen, though, I may be your chairperson but I sure don't like praying out loud in front of groups. Makes me so nervous and anxious I can't think! That would definitely be my prayer roadblock, why I don't pray more. Does anyone else have that one?"

A chorus of voices agreed.

"Mine is the same as Claire's," Arlen disclosed. "My aunt used to say that if I would only become more spiritually mature, I would be more comfortable and confident doing that. Instead, sometimes I even skip church gatherings if I suspect we might be asked to suddenly pray something spontaneously out loud, not reading from a book or page. Sure, people like Pastor Milton are gifted with beautiful words to pray up front or in groups—so let him do it, not me. If I'm not spiritually mature enough to pray out loud the way I should, that's definitely my prayer roadblock."

Luciana looked confessionally at her colleagues. "I pray, but usually it's talking to God throughout the day's activities. It could be when I'm wheeling the grocery cart through the store, cleaning the house, walking through our neighborhood or especially when I lie down to sleep at night. It seems like here at the church, we've had classes or meetings where we expect members to come sit around tables for prayer. They've always been poorly attended, though. We've concluded our people must not believe prayer is that important, because they don't show up for that kind of thing. But now as we discuss prayer roadblocks, maybe a lot of people are like me. Sitting and praying around a table with others just isn't my preferred 'prayer posture,' you could call it. I like movement, walking or even cooking or shopping or something, while I pray."

Ebony shook her head sadly. "My prayer roadblock would be that I don't always feel God's presence when I pray. And if I can't feel God is there, it means God isn't listening—correct? So that's why, even though I believe prayer makes a difference, I don't pray much."

One by one, each leader named a prayer roadblock. Jeffrey waited until last to share his.

"Now hear me when I agree that it's obvious our membership thinks reciting prayers at church is important and all. But me personally? Well, my mother died when I was only seven years old, even though a Sunday school teacher at the time told me if I would pray for her, God would heal her. I did pray, and God didn't. So, I learned the bitter, difficult lesson at a young age, growing up without a mom, that prayers don't really matter. They're only nice words that may help people feel better in some way. To be transparent with you, we don't try to pray our way along on this leadership team, if that's what you're getting at. We don't need to anyway. We have plenty of expertise and skill on the team ourselves to handle everything that's needed for the church."

"But do you really?" I wondered aloud. "Is Faith Church really just the same as any community civic organization? With you leaders on board to manage and maintain it, keep it financially solvent, figure out how to adequately fill the membership rolls and assign everyone a duty, plus engineer a canned food drive every Christmas for the needy? If you already know what to do and how do it, why has the church continued to be plateaued and now starting some decline on your leadership watch?"

The leadership team was silent.

It seemed now an opportune moment to introduce them to the summons of the "open road" I already explained to you in the previous chapter. And how it eventually also dawned on Jesus' first traveling companions on the journey together that their own extensive experience and talents alone weren't enough. And that a generous measure of an additional miraculous ingredient they finally asked Jesus to teach them was required in order to shift from ministry managers to bold, adventurous Jesus followers on world changing adventure.

I concluded with this. "As you will recognize from scripture, it was the short breakthrough prayer Jesus taught them—*Your Will Be Done.* Here's my expanded version of it:

God, may your preferred will break through, change history, usher in and accomplish through us your new hopes, dreams and possibilities—both in the life of our church, and in our own lives. We surrender our wills for yours, in order to fully follow you. Amen.

"Jesus taught his followers both then and now to add this to the prayer we already offer to God the Comforter, God the Sympathizer, God the Healer and God the Protector. Just think—the new additional prayer ingredient is praying to God the Almighty—the Creator of heaven and earth. The One who longs to do, as the book of Ephesians says, 'infinitely more than what we can ask or imagine, according to his power that works within us' (Ephesians 3:20, ISV).

"You see, prayers asking for God's breakthroughs activate God's power and passion within each of us. Those who pray regularly for God's new possibilities and open doors find themselves habitually looking up and out with holy expectation. And as we set aside our own preferences in order to make room for God's, our hearts and minds then have space to discern and pursue God's next steps forward. In fact, God's future for us becomes irresistible."

After a long pause, chairperson Claire spoke. "So, you are suggesting our church has been behaving more like we're just managing our logistics, rather than like a spiritual movement? With the ingredient of asking God to break through with new possibilities in and through everything, praying that prayer, at the center of it all? And really expecting and believing it will make a difference—the difference we so desperately need? This makes me nervous."

Arlen looked thoughtful. "Yes, that's a new picture to try to wrap ourselves around. Good heavens, that would change everything. I mean, we would have to change everything. Reorganize the way we handle our leadership meetings, and what we do at our meetings. Adjust the way we think about making prayer a priority, and how we pray in general. We would also have to somehow get the congregation engaged in praying more, too. Hmmm—would it require us to all pray out loud? What if we didn't feel anything, didn't feel God's presence when we were praying? Would that mean God wasn't listening?"

"Listen, this could be a legitimate new approach for us to try," Ben urged. "Because if we keep doing what we've always done, nothing different for our church will ever happen. But we leaders would have to find our way past some of our own prayer roadblocks we've named, so we could get freed up to approach prayer more fully. If we could only do that, just imagine what might be in store!"

"Definitely agreed," I assured them. "I have a 'Prayer Roadblocks Removal Guide' to provide you for learning and discussion on that very issue. Finding release from the most common prayer roadblocks can happen more easily than you might expect."

"Are there other reasons it makes you nervous to think about, Claire and everyone?" Leland questioned. "Is it because our plans would be out of our hands, and be in God's hands instead? Let's admit it, we are used to controlling what happens at the church ourselves. I'm sure this doesn't mean we devalue the work we've previously done to ground ourselves in our mission, vision and basic business practices for Faith Church. But now all that valuable foundational investment would rightly become a launching pad for what's next, rather than us thinking that it's enough on its own to move the church forward. Adding the breakthrough prayer from Jesus really could become some kind of adventure!"

As further discussion unfolded among them, Faith Church's leadership began to create on a chart what they referred to as their shared "what if...?" prayer covenant:

- **What if** — we covenant together to actively believe with our lives (even those among us who aren't completely sure yet) that prayer makes a difference? And after praying, we behave accordingly by looking "up and out" expectantly to notice, name and celebrate God's responses we trust to unfold, according to God's time frame?

- **What if** — we individually and collectively refuse to let past personal prayers God didn't fulfill to our specifications be a roadblock now for willingness to experiment with prayers inviting new possibilities to break through?

- **What if** — we hold each other accountable to together reformat our leadership meetings and responsibilities into prayer-filled, expectant leadership of a living, growing movement rather than as an administrative structure managing an organization in decline?

- **What if** — we develop a simple daily prayer practice in our own personal prayer lives and also when we gather as the leadership team, asking for God's discernment for our next future steps, instead of only requesting God to bless our self-generated plans?

- **What if** — we model all this ourselves, and likewise eventually train the entire congregation to put the missing ingredient of prayer for breakthroughs of new possibilities and open doors into their own daily prayer practices--so all of us are praying together as the signature ingredient of the spiritual movement named Faith Church?

At the end of the future focus session, it was Jeffrey who unexpectedly proposed that the leadership council begin by adopting a short breakthrough prayer he had customized from mine, and that they should each pray it daily at breakfast. "We might as well test God, and see if God will do anything!" he admitted.

God, please break through and open doors to new hopes and possibilities for our church and in our own lives...and we will surrender and faithfully follow Christ onto the open road adventure of Your new and unknown future. May Your will be done. Amen!

Are you wondering what happened there next? Over the next weeks, it was as if the leadership team's figurative door to the future began to swing open and they caught a first whiff of the fresh, invitational air of the spiritual open road. They made the commitment to live into their "What if...?" covenant both during time spent together, as well as individually through personal study and reflection time in between. To be sure, their conversions of perspective didn't happen overnight. The transformation for some involved discontinuing both a few limiting prayer roadblocks and a few limiting "organization mindset" behaviors. Sooner than the leaders at the pivotal future focus session would have ever expected, Faith Church found itself beginning to advance.

The Faith Church leadership team did utilize the "Prayer Roadblocks Removal" discussion guide that I'll include here next for you and your team's use. They found it so permission-giving that Pastor Milton shared it with the entire congregation one Sunday morning, explaining it during his sermon time. That freed many to get on common ground when it came to understanding a few key prayer basics. And when the churchwide Breakthrough Prayer Initiative was later launched, the congregation was ready. The shift from "organization" to "movement" had liftoff.

What is a Breakthrough Prayer Initiative?

Glad you asked, because we're going there next. In chapter 3, I'll provide you a full explanation, plus a step-by-step Breakthrough Prayer Initiative "Wayfinder" guide to help you move yours into place across the entire life of your congregation.

Then, after that, in chapter 4, you'll learn about more specific breakthrough prayer practices to incorporate when helpful for the unanticipated, unexpected challenges and surprises you may encounter along your open road expedition following Jesus. They're perfect to have packed along, so you can be ready to pull out the breakthrough prayer practice that fits best.

Discussion/Reflection Questions

1. What stood out to you in this chapter? To which comments from persons on the Faith Church leadership team, if any, could you most relate? Explain.

2. Would you describe yourself as someone who has an intellectual belief that prayer matters, or are you a person who actively believes that prayer makes a difference? Share at least one reason for your response.

3. Have you been more prone as a church leader to think of your congregation as an organization whose logistics you feel responsible to maintain, or as a movement of Christ followers who together comprise a courageous, active spiritual movement spreading through your community? How has your concept of your church tended to dictate your enthusiastic hope, or weariness and challenge, as you attend and serve?

4. Look at the Prayer "Roadblock Removal" guide in the next section (it's the same one that the Faith Church leaders utilized), then discuss together. Is there anything you need to unlearn/learn about prayer? Which roadblock removal could give you more freedom for investment in your personal prayer life?

5. What is your reaction to the proposal of intentionally adding a daily prayer, both personally and collectively, asking God to break through anew and open new doors? What do you anticipate would happen, if anything?

6. If you are using this book as a resource for your team, you are invited to try adding the short breakthrough prayer Jeffrey crafted to your daily prayer lives for a time period of your choosing. Keep notes on what you see and notice God doing in response, both in your own lives and in the life of your church. At your future team meetings, make certain to plan a time for each to report back, in order to be strengthened in your prayer practice and to celebrate God's living and active presence!

Prayer: "Roadblock Removals" Guide

Perhaps you are most accustomed to prayer typically taking place at church during the weekly worship service, at church meetings to open and close, on behalf of a congregational prayer chain list of needs, or when saying grace over a meal.

The prospect of infusing a churchwide Breakthrough Prayer Initiative within your leadership team and across your congregation to unleash Holy-Spirit led movement forward may seem unsettling in some ways. Often that's because of self-limiting assumptions we or others have believed about prayer that have held us back.

Hopefully the following prayer approach roadblock removals will help set you, and those you lead, at ease, and unite you in your new ongoing priority of prayer. This list is not meant to be comprehensive. It is simply a place for you to start with honest discussion and reflection about your own prayer life thus far, and how you might experiment with living into it differently.

See what God may want to do to free you and your entire church when it comes to prayer, the essential ingredient that ignites the vitality of the body of Christ, the Church!

Instructions. Read, reflect and discuss each of these. Which seems to provide the most helpful insights for you, for your leadership team, and for your church?

PRAYER "ROADBLOCK" REMOVALS[1]

- *Silent prayer versus spoken prayer.* Many shy away from attending group prayer because they fear they'll be requested to pray out loud. It's permission-giving to let everyone know that God welcomes and hears all prayer, whether it utilizes spoken words or is offered silently. Romans 8:26 reminds us that "the Spirit comes to help our weakness. We don't know what we should pray, but the Spirit himself pleads our case with unexpressed groans." Both prayer with and without words is equally valid.

- *General versus specific prayer.* Some churchgoers avoid additional involvement in prayer because they feel uncertain what to pray for. Granted, one obviously prays very specifically about an illness or a crisis. Prayer aimed and targeted thus could be nicknamed *Archer's Prayer.*

---

[1] Kibbey, Sue Nilson. Adapted from *Floodgates: Holy Momentum for a Fearless Church,* Abingdon Press, 2016.

But members may be unsure how to pray about other situations. The permission-giving good news is that Jesus himself taught his disciples how to pray using the general prayer of "Your kingdom come, your will be done, on earth as it is in heaven" (Matt 6:10 NIV). In fact, "Your will be done" is known as the prayer that never fails! That kind of general prayer—what you pray when you don't know what to pray—connects with the heart of God just as specific prayer does. *Threshold Prayer* is generalized prayer: prayerfully lifting everything to the threshold of God's miraculous grace, and asking God to do what only the Almighty desires to do.

- *Touch versus no-touch prayer.* The Gospels clearly describe the Holy Spirit's supernatural activity through touch, the laying on of hands with prayer for healing, anointing with oil, and more. Jesus and his disciples used touch as they prayed for those around them, as did the leaders in the early church throughout the rest of the New Testament. However, there may be those in your congregation whose personal life histories have involved physical abuse that has left emotional scars, and they would prefer not to be touched during prayer. God's Spirit can work powerfully with or without touch. Assure that permission to touch is optional in your Breakthrough Prayer Initiative so that all may feel comfortable.

- ***Lights-on/lights-off prayer.*** It seems easy, even natural, to pray when life is good, things are going well, and you're seated by a window with a gorgeous view of the beauty of nature. You feel God's presence as you pray, and that intuitive sense reassures you that God is there. But what about those times when you feel nothing when you pray? There seems to be no Holy Spirit awareness around you. You wonder if God heard you. Does my prayer matter? you ask yourself. *Why pray at all, if I don't feel God close at hand when I do?*

Mother Teresa, legendary minister to the poor, left her life's journals behind when she died in 1997. Although she also left instructions for them to be destroyed, ten years later a book of her personal letters was published that shocked the world.[2] They revealed that her prayer life for many years had been "dark"—without any sense of the light or hint of God's tangible presence. Yet Mother Teresa always continued to pray, even in what she felt were years of unemotional, blank darkness. And in hindsight it's evident that God continued to work consistently and faithfully in and through her prayers.

---

[2] Mother Teresa: *Come Be My Light: The Private Writings of the Saint of Calcutta,* ed. Brian Kolodiejchuk, Doubleday, 2007.

It's crucial for those who pray to keep this awareness: there will be times of prayer that feel full of God's light and presence—*lights-on prayer*—as well as times when no tangible presence of God can be sensed, *lights-off prayer*. God, however, is equally attentive during both. Continue to pray whether the "light" of God's presence feels on or off. As the Psalmist wrote, "Even when I walk through the darkest valley, I fear no danger because you are with me" (Ps 23:4).

My Notes

1. I have struggled at times, or consistently, with the following prayer roadblocks:

2. The roadblock removal I most need to apply to experience greater freedom when I pray is:

CHAPTER THREE

Breakthrough Prayer Initiative *Wayfinder*

You've already equipped your leadership team with a short breakthrough prayer for daily use both personally and collectively. At your team's meetings, you now have begun including report-back opportunities to share about new breakthroughs each may have noticed. In this chapter, I intend to provide you instructions that will serve as your wider strategy for bringing the miraculous simple prayer ingredient I've described to the heart of your church's culture and identity ongoing.

By the term "wayfinder" I mean the key markers to orientate and navigate along your open road expedition's Breakthrough Prayer Initiative implementation route. Let's begin with a definition.

Oswald Chambers, author of the classic devotional *My Utmost for His Highest,* emphasized that just as our physical bodies require physical food in order to stay healthy, strong, active and energetic, so the Church — which scripture calls the body of Christ — requires the "food" of prayer. Otherwise, is it any wonder that some churches become complacent, listless, weak, uninterested in much of any activity—and can even die? That's what takes place if a church is only "snacking" on prayer, rather than "feasting" on prayer.

What is a *Breakthrough Prayer Initiative?*

This is a term I've coined to describe a congregation-wide drive engaging the vast majority of attendees, from preschoolers through senior adults, to activate their existing prayer lives by adding one more miraculous ingredient.

A Breakthrough Prayer Initiative is not an emphasis for a week or for a month of church life, or only an extra effort to make during the pastor's prayer sermon series. It's not another program to add, nor is it to be assigned exclusively to a committee or task force to perform. It's not just for members, while church leaders instead focus their efforts on building repairs and administration. And it's certainly not for the pastor or other dedicated leader to carry on alone on behalf of the flock!

A Breakthrough Prayer initiative is an *all-church practice*. It's the practice of everyone, all ages, always adding this ingredient to their prayers offered both individually and also collectively as teams, small groups or other ministry gatherings. The choir, women's circles, youth group, food pantry volunteers — everyone. Church leaders are out front, modeling and championing the practice themselves. And let's emphasize yet again, it's ongoing.

Why add this prayer ingredient? It always bears repeating. Just as we are accustomed to pray to God the Comforter and Sympathizer when we offer prayers for those who are grieving, troubled or in crisis; just as we pray to God the Healer when we pray for those who are sick or suffering; just as we pray to God the Protector when we ask God to keep safe those who are traveling or whose lives might be at risk; a Breakthrough Prayer Initiative trains everyone to add a potent prayer request to God the Almighty to break through in our church and in our own lives with new hopes and possibilities.

The moment God's people pray, God begins a response. Praying is our part for sure. But prayer is *two-way* communication, which also includes now encouraging everyone to pay attention, to look and listen for God's guidance and new doors opening via whatever methodology and on whatever Divine time frame it may come. Perhaps through a new circumstance that unfolds? Unanticipated provision? An insight, conviction of heart, or idea that could only be authored by the Holy Spirit? A new fire in your (or someone else's) belly for an innovative way to spread the message and love of Jesus? We serve an endlessly creative God whose response we might miss, if we mistakenly think a Breakthrough Prayer Initiative is one-sided, only having the congregation memorize and repeat a new short prayer together. That could quickly become an empty "word habit of the mind."

So, let's get started on how you could begin.

Wayfinder #1. Identify or craft a short breakthrough prayer to introduce for your congregation's use.

Here is a breakthrough prayer example you could adopt or customize:

God, please break through and open doors to new hopes, dreams and possibilities for our church and in our own lives...and we will surrender and faithfully follow Christ onto the open road adventure of Your new and unknown future. May Your will be done. Amen!

Or if you prefer, your leadership team could create one that uniquely fits your congregation. Here are a few practical guidelines, learned from others who have traversed this Wayfinder before you.

- Remember that the breakthrough prayer is only a **short additive component** to the existing prayers of your church — so it should be short. At the most, two sentences are a user-friendly length. Some churches have created an effective single sentence breakthrough prayer, or even just a few words that are easy to remember and internalize.

- **Do not create a comprehensive prayer** that also includes everything the church is already praying about (the world, the country's leaders, our own discipleship, the needs of the community, etc.), and then weave the short breakthrough prayer component within all that. If you do, the congregation may look at the lengthy new prayer you introduce as nothing distinctive, only one more prayer to read together, like all the others. And they will likely miss the new prayer for breakthroughs component entirely.

- **Use specific action verb phrases** in your breakthrough prayer that invite God to break through with the "new"— such as open wide, blow afresh, shine new light, reveal new pathways, throw wide, burst open, unlatch, release, expand, unfurl, overflow. The language of the breakthrough prayer matters. If your language is ambiguous, vague or complicated, your congregation will not be able to notice and name what God is doing in response when you ask.

- Prayers for ourselves to grow deeper in our faith or for God to bless and care for us and loved ones are important — but remember, most already pray for that. Keep reminding yourselves that your breakthrough prayer component to add is to be different — not just about us.

Wayfinder #2. Plan how you will equip your attendees with the new short breakthrough prayer component in written form.

It's often placed on a small business-sized card and distributed for easy reference throughout the day, or provided to everyone electronically in a format appropriate to download as the wallpaper or desktop on your smartphone, tablet or computer—as a visual reminder to pray.

A few other creative examples invented to keep the breakthrough prayer handy for the hearts and minds of the entire congregation include:

- **Laminate the breakthrough prayer card,** punch a hole and attach a rubber band — and it has suddenly become perfect to hang in your shower so you can pray while getting ready each morning.

- **Set the short breakthrough prayer to music,** and invite a talented musician to sing/play a recording that can be downloaded. You can also sing the prayer in unison during worship. Having it set to music helps it to "play" again and again in the minds of those who've heard it.

- Along with the breakthrough prayer on the small card, **add a photo or image** that uniquely represents your setting or mission field. One church, located just a block from Lake Superior, placed a dramatic photo of the waves crashing on the nearby shore on their prayer card. They customized the wording of their prayer: "Just as the waves break upon the shoreline of our city, God, we ask you to break anew upon our lives and our church with dreams and possibilities beyond what we can think of ourselves...."

  Another church, located for many years right next to an active railroad track upon which trains passed frequently, put the image of a train on their breakthrough prayer card—and their prayer incorporated that theme: "God, we ask you to show us new tracks to a new future of your choosing, not ours...."

- Numerous churches have had their short breakthrough prayer printed on **inexpensive rubber wrist bracelets** instead of using cards, so that it could be worn and seen more conveniently to remember to pray. (Remember to order child's bracelet sizes, too!)

- **Consider using a symbol** to drive home any image inherent in the wording of your breakthrough prayer. One congregation's was worded to ask the wind of God's Spirit to twirl anew the spirit of the congregation with courage to discover hope-filled next steps. They put the breakthrough prayer on a small card that featured a pinwheel photo — and then attached prayer cards to actual small pinwheels that were handed out to the congregation after worship on a beautiful spring morning. As people exited outside, the breeze twirled the colorful pinwheels — and many said later it gave them a vivid metaphor of what God longed to do with them through their breakthrough prayer.

Wayfinder #3. Introduce the Breakthrough Prayer Initiative and distribute the prayer to your congregation.

Make sure your leadership team has first established the breakthrough prayer in your daily and collective prayer lives together, and has already established it as part of your prayer practice — so that you are leading by example. It is impossible to expect the congregation to do more or go further spiritually than we are ourselves.

Then choose an occasion when the entire church family can receive your initial introduction to the Breakthrough Prayer Initiative, including children and teens, the homebound, and those who may live in another part of the state or country during certain seasons. It may be during a live worship service, online, in the church newsletter/e-letter—or hopefully all of these and more, since repetition is crucial. Have your church's additive breakthrough prayer ready to distribute in whatever written form as you prefer (see Wayfinder #2 for ideas) at that time.

The Breakthrough Prayer Initiative may be presented and explained by your pastor, or a church leader who is passionate about its addition to personal and church-wide prayer life in order to receive God's discernment for what's next.

Need ideas on what you might say in your introduction and explanation? Here's potential content gathered for you, so that you can choose what you like and to paraphrase into your own words:

Prayer has always been important to our church. We have worship service prayer, prayer chain prayer, and table grace prayer. We have prayer to open and close our meetings. And now, at this crucial time in the life of our church when we are seeking God's guidance for our future, church leadership would like to introduce a new potent prayer component to include in our prayers—both personally and all together. We call it our new "breakthrough prayer."

It doesn't replace our existing prayers—it is an additive piece. Now is not a time to pull back on prayers of any kind. Instead, we need more! This is one that the leadership team has already added to our own prayer practices, and we'd like to invite the entire congregation into a church-wide "Breakthrough Prayer Initiative." Let me explain the details.

Just as we are already accustomed to pray to God the Comforter and Sympathizer when we offer prayers for those who are grieving, troubled or in crisis; just as we already pray to God the Healer when we pray for those who are sick or suffering; just as we already pray to God the Protector when we ask God to keep safe those who are traveling or whose lives might be at risk; a Breakthrough Prayer Initiative trains everyone to add a prayer request to God the Almighty.

Our short additive breakthrough prayer request

*to the Almighty is based on what Jesus taught
his disciples to pray (Matthew 6:9-10):*

> *God, please break through and open doors to new
> hopes, dreams and possibilities for our church
> and in our own lives...and we will surrender
> and faithfully follow Christ onto the open road
> adventure of Your new and unknown future.
> May Your will be done. Amen! (or insert your
> own breakthrough prayer you've created here).*

*Have you noticed? It's easy for our usual
prayers to become inward-focused only-on
ourselves, our loved ones, on wanting God's
blessings upon what we are already doing
here, or on our own opinions about what
should happen next at church. But when
we add prayer inviting God the Almighty to
miraculously break through, open new doors,
and usher in new possibilities-and when we
are willing to surrender our own wills and
preferences to make room for God's, everything
can change! We will begin looking up and out
expectantly for what God might show us next,
rather than "down and in" with discouragement or passivity.*

The moment God's people pray, God begins a

response. Praying is our part for sure. But prayer is two-way communication, so we also need to begin encouraging each other to pay attention, to look and listen for God's guidance and notice new doors opening via whatever methodology and on whatever Divine time frame it may come. Perhaps it may be through a new circumstance that unfolds? Unanticipated provision? An insight, conviction of heart, or idea that could only be authored by the Holy Spirit?

And the new breakthrough prayer addition is not only for our church as a whole. It's also for you personally. When any of us surrender and empty ourselves of our own longtime, maybe even stubborn perspectives and opinions that fill us, we create spiritual space inside for God to birth anew in you. Maybe new fire in your belly for an innovative way to spread the message and love of Jesus? A unique calling to serve that will bring you joy and fulfillment? A dawning solution to a personal challenge or situation you hadn't had spiritual room inside (or openness) to receive before?

Let's be clear. We serve an endlessly creative God whose prayer responses we might miss, if we mistakenly assume a Breakthrough Prayer Initiative is just having the congregation memorize and repeat a new short prayer together. That for us could quickly become an empty "word habit of the mind." And that's not the intention for this new congregational breakthrough prayer.

Do you really believe prayer makes a difference? Not just a belief that prayer matters, but an active, confident trust that your prayers invite God to bring new directional discernment that will both transform your life and instigate new movement forward of our church? Enough that the invitation to add this breakthrough prayer to your daily prayer life sounds exciting and just what we all need? If yes, what motivation this is for all of us to move prayer to the center of everything!

A movement of Jesus, the Church, is fueled anew again and again by prayers for God's new yet-un-imagined possibilities to open before us, and our ongoing surrender to relinquish our human plans in order to act on our discernment of the Divine's guidance. This is our time. Let's go!

Additional notes for Wayfinder #3:

- Immediately distribute the churchwide breakthrough prayer after it is introduced, and **pray it together immediately.**

- Consider proposing a **daily time** to invite everyone to pray it together, wherever you find yourselves. Some churches have suggested a time that could be convenient either in the morning or evening (for example, 8 a.m. or 8 p.m. daily) to accommodate busy schedules. Fuel this by inviting persons to take a "selfie" photo wherever they might be at home, in the community or beyond, when they are praying the breakthrough prayer—and post it on the church's social media, or send it to the pastor to share during worship or other congregational occasions together. Another version of this idea has been to invite persons to video themselves (and maybe their children or spouse or friends with them) praying the breakthrough prayer "on location" wherever they are. What an awareness this brings that our congregation is regularly blanketing our "world" with prayers for new possibilities!

- Emphasize again and again to the congregation that the **breakthrough prayer practice also includes looking up and out with expectation to notice and name the breakthroughs,** open doors and new discernment of God's divine responses. Encourage this aspect of the new breakthrough prayer practice by creating a "Notice and Name

Your Breakthroughs" card, or online form on your website or other means, and continually invite yourselves and your congregation to share what they see happening personally and in the life of the church. If you are utilizing the open road or greatest expedition theme, you could call this a "Trail Magic" card—since that's the term trail hikers use to describe the provision of unexpected resources and assistance along the journey.

Be sure to **share the breakthrough stories** both large and small, ongoing, with the congregation. All of us are motivated to pray more as we hear about and celebrate answered prayers.

- Within the first month after introducing and launching your Breakthrough Prayer Initiative, consider scheduling a sermon time or other occasion when your pastor or a church leader can bring the entire congregation the insights summarized on the **"Prayer Roadblocks Removal" guide** that was included with chapter 2. When members begin to pray the breakthrough prayer regularly, they may discover they have a prayer roadblock or two—and this could help free them to embrace the adventure of prayer more fully.

Wayfinder #4. Integrate the Breakthrough Prayer Initiative widely throughout the life of the church, all ages.

Did you know that there's more to weaving your

Breakthrough Prayer Initiative through all aspects, beyond simply including it as a unison prayer in worship? Let's take a look at a range of opportunities you may consider.

Worship Services. Whether you are worshiping in person or online, including the congregation-wide breakthrough prayer is indeed a wonderful emphasis. That is, when it's prayed together—not sometimes, but every time—your pastor or other church leader always explains beforehand what the breakthrough prayer is, and why we are praying it. Otherwise, it can quickly become a weekly rote recitation—and those attending may not even particularly remember later whether or not they prayed it that day or perhaps they are a first-time guest.

Imagine ahead of time that you are introducing the breakthrough prayer to a group of people who have never heard of it before, and have no concept of asking God to break through anew. (In so doing, you are also reminding the congregation again and again why we are praying this prayer.) Here's an example of what you might repeat each time:

If you've never worshiped with our church before, a good first thing to know about us is that we believe in the power of prayer, that prayer really does make a difference. So much so that we've crafted

*a special short prayer specifically asking God to
break through anew with miraculous possibilities,
open doors and fresh direction for our church and
in our own personal lives. We call it our breakthrough prayer, we pray this together every week in
worship, and we also all pray it individually every
day. We know that surrendering our own desires
and preferences in order to make room for what
God can bring is crucial, so we pray that as well.
If you happen to be worshiping with us today and
you need a breakthrough of any kind, this prayer
may be for you. And you can be confident and trust
that God loves the invitation to open new doors and
lead the church, as well as each of us, in miraculous
new ways. Let's pray together now* ... (and then lead
everyone in the breakthrough prayer).

Make sure to have extra written cards with the
breakthrough prayer printed for first-time guest
distribution.

**Breakthrough prayer candles in worship/
online worship.** Consider the option during
worship of lighting candles that represent specific
persons or situations that need a breakthrough of
any kind—named or unnamed. If worshiping in
person, you might place a bank of votive candles up
near the altar along with a lighter. Before or during
the worship service, explain that if anyone knows
of someone or something needing a God-provided
breakthrough, you are invited to come forward and

light a votive candle. At the end of the service your pastor or a leader could stand next to the bank of lit candles and pray a general prayer for all at once, inviting God to bring newness, discernment and life to each. If worshiping online, invite persons to have a candle set before them—and to light their candles if there's a circumstance or person for which they request special prayer. Then you can pray a "blanket" breakthrough prayer for who or what's represented by lit candles remotely.

At church meetings, gatherings, classes, music/choir rehearsals and on serving teams. Take the Breakthrough Prayer Initiative for your church beyond worship and into every occasion when God's people gather.

- Ensure that every committee chair, youth group sponsor, choir director, Sunday school teacher, worship band leader all have the church's breakthrough prayer handy on a small card or electronically.

- Encourage them to always begin their group by not only asking for prayer concerns as may be usual, but also asking who has noticed a prayer breakthrough of any size either at church or personally—and invite it to be shared.

- Suggest to the leaders that they should arrive with a prayer breakthrough themselves to share if they've discerned one, in order to demonstrate how to notice and name what God is doing that's new.

- One church reported that they refer to this opening segment as "Pows and Wows." Each person gathered is given the opportunity to share their brief answers to these questions:

  How has life landed you a POW of any sort this week or month?

  How has our breakthrough God blessed you with a new WOW this week or month?

Prayer Walking. Prayer postures—whether we are sitting, standing or moving—can make a difference in prayer engagement. (Remember Luciana back at Faith Church?) In fact, engaging your leadership team and your entire congregation by walking while praying is a highly effective prayer posture for connecting a large swath of people to pray together.

At your leadership team meetings, if meeting in person, plan that the first ten minutes of your time you will choose a room or space in your building or on your church's property to **walk through together, praying silently** (or aloud, as per individual preference) for God to bless and anoint that space and those who will utilize it with fresh faith, new hope and courage to embrace and follow Christ. Likewise, invite the church meetings and other gatherings just mentioned in the previous bullet point to use the first ten minutes for the same. What might God unleash, if the choir invested their first ten minutes of rehearsal time to walk and pray through the choir loft—asking God to use their music as a vehicle to speak deeply to the congregation's hearts and spirits the coming Sunday? What might God unfold, if the youth group walked and prayed across the empty parking lot and asked God to fill it with cars of new people who desperately need the good news and love of Jesus?

During or at the end of worship, consider leading the congregation out the sanctuary doors (do not just try to send them without you!) to pray and walk around the church, or to pray and walk through your church's space for children and youth, or other location. Ask everyone to pray silently for God to fill and overflow it with such love and peace that each life touched would experience transformation.

If your congregation is not able to gather in your building to pray and walk together, an excellent alternate option developed by some churches is to provide the congregation with a floor plan of your church building—either on paper, or downloadable from your church website. Invite everyone to do a **virtual prayer walk** through your building, using the floor plan for a guide. The work and ministry that usually happens in your church's spaces can be Holy Spirit-saturated through congregational praying and walking, whether or not you're physically on site.

Children love the Breakthrough Prayer Initiative, too! Remember to include the children who are part of your congregation, who may show themselves to be even more responsive than adults with praying for breakthroughs and then naming what they see God doing. Children enjoy praying and walking as part of their Sunday class time or vacation Bible school, and appreciate having a children's breakthrough prayer to learn themselves if the wording of the church's is a bit beyond them. If you craft one for kids, remember to include active "breakthrough" language just as you have done for the churchwide breakthrough prayer. "Jesus loves me" or "God loves everyone and so do I" are appropriate truths for children, but statements like this are not breakthrough prayers. Keep in mind that you have the opportunity to train up young world changers who deeply believe in the power of prayer, and equip them thus.

Wayfinder #5. Multiply impact by user-friendly additional prayer adventures.

The ideal fabric of the life of a follower of Jesus is that prayer would be integrated not only in church life together, but also throughout day-to-day life. Every leadership team does well to continually imagine answers to "What's next?" for members and their prayer practices beyond the church doors. Here are several simple ideas gathered from other churches like yours.

- **Prayer stations in your home.** During the COVID-19 pandemic when one congregation could only worship online rather than in person, the pastor used one week's sermon to invite parishioners to set up a simple prayer station in each room of their home. She suggested moving from prayer station to prayer station once each day, using the prayer station reminders as a catalyst to pray for breakthroughs of various kinds. The pastor then, via the video feed of her smartphone, virtually toured viewers through her own house to point out each prayer station she'd created. In one room it was on a dresser where framed photos of family members stood as her prayer focus. In the kitchen, it was a prayer cross nestled in a mixing bowl that served as her prayer station to pray for the wide mixture of diverse persons in the congregation, and for God's renewing grace to fill each with new peace and hope during the pandemic season. After showing her entire home prayer station circuit as an example, she invited everyone to invent their own home prayer stations to enhance personal prayer life—and to send her photos or videos she could share. Many reported later that setting up home prayer stations was an idea that deeply energized their prayer lives.

- **Prayer words.** Keep interest high in the journey of personal prayer by choosing a month in which each person receives a unique "prayer word" – and is invited to use it each day in their prayers, asking God to break through anew in and through that prayer word. Churches have printed "prayer words" on cards for members to draw from a basket in live worship, and to take home with them—or else emailed a list of prayer words to their home-quarantined congregation and invited them to choose one to use for the month. At month's end, everyone is encouraged to share breakthroughs and new insights that have come through their particular prayer word. Prayer word ideas are many—and might include Hope, Expectancy, Wait, Ascend, Trust, Discern among many other choices.

- **Egg Timers: the use of symbols.** In response to his congregation's frequent complaint that they loved the church's new breakthrough prayer, but never seemed to have enough time daily to pray more, one pastor decided to try something new for day-to-day prayer practice enhancement. The first Sunday of Lent, a small plastic 5-minute egg timer (hourglass-shaped, inexpensively purchased online) was gifted to each member present. The pastor invited them to find just five minutes daily to sit with a notebook, pen and the egg timer, pray "Speak, Lord, your servant is listening...." then turn over the egg timer, be still and listen spiritually for God's voice—jotting down anything they sensed. He pointed out that most people squeeze in daily moments to offer their prayer requests to God, but don't take an additional few prayer minutes to discern God's response.

The pastor's idea was for the congregation to commit for the entire season of Lent to this practice, as an experiment to remedy the "no time for prayer" complaint from so many. So many breakthrough stories were shared during and after the Lenten season that most members continued the daily egg timer prayer practice far beyond Easter.

Would you have ever guessed that a mechanism or symbol so simple would bring such positive prayer impact? What other symbols come to mind you might likewise use to enhance prayer lives?

- **Personal prayer walking (or driving) route in your neighborhood or community.** One church in a small community set up a summer "breakthrough prayer route" for its members, identifying town landmarks along the way to stop and pray for civil servants (the courthouse), essential workers (the police station, the fire-house, and the hospital), the next generation (the elementary, middle and high school buildings) and serving the needs of our neighbors (the church facility itself). The entire walk route was approximately two miles, and simple booklets were created so persons could tally their walks for three months. At the end of the summer, everyone who had completed the prayer walk route at least once received a donated tee shirt with the church's name and "Breakthrough Prayer Makes a Difference!" on the front. The majority of members got a tee shirt, and the times the prayer route had been walked overall totaled more than 300. Is it any surprise that the vitality of that church surged forward in the fall, as God continued to show the congregation more ways to pray for, to love and to serve its community?

Similarly, a church nestled in a rural area with no surrounding neighborhood of houses or businesses designed a several-mile prayer drive route, also featuring area landmarks (the library, the factory where many local citizens were employed, the grain elevator) where members were encouraged to stop and pray.

Wayfinder #6. Always/Never Words to the Wise—for sustaining Breakthrough Prayer Initiative momentum.

By now, your leadership team and congregation are underway. You are in the intentional process of shaping your church's culture and heart-level identity—your congregational DNA—around the practice of ongoing breakthrough prayer.

From learnings shared by many other Breakthrough Prayer Initiative churches, here's trial-and-error-learned advice for sustaining its impetus.

Always when you are planning any new activity, ministry or event for your church, put "How will breakthrough prayer be incorporated?" as a non-negotiable element to be included—the same way refreshments, name tags or other arrangements might be. Will it be prayer walking the space or location ahead of time with a large group of people, asking God to break through anew in the lives of those who will be involved? What creative approach to allowing breakthrough prayer to impact might your planning team imagine?

Here are two examples, to get your ideation started:

- At a church that annually gifted every third grade student with a Bible, the entire church leadership team gathered a few days before and held every Bible, praying by name for the student who would receive it and asking God to open their hearts for new faith and trust in Christ.

- At a church that provided backpacks of school supplies to a neighborhood elementary school each fall, leaders additionally met with the principal and asked for a "first name only" list of the students' names. Each name was then printed on a white label sticker, and placed on an unsharpened pencil. At the start of fall, church members were invited to pick up one or more of the pencils, and to use them as "pencil prayer" reminders to pray for the students with those names. Rather than simply giving school supplies, the congregation also gave the life-changing gift of prayer.

Always remember to adjust your short breakthrough prayer periodically, to keep it fresh and relevant for your leadership and the congregation as its seasons change. It's not recommended to change the breakthrough prayer too frequently—but it is important to reinvent it occasionally. When you do, always remember to continue including an up-and-out action verb with imagery that is specific enough for pray-ers to discern when God is responding to the prayer. And keep to the rule of keeping it short—two sentences or less. It is meant to be a short, powerful additive element to the overall prayer life of the congregation.

When, specifically, might you **change up** your church's breakthrough prayer? Here are a few examples.

- To coordinate with a new worship sermon series

- To enhance a new church season such as Advent or Lent

- At the launch of a new step forward for the church, or to prepare specifically for it

- When new persons are rotating into church leadership roles, and are embracing the call to lead your movement.

Always encourage, support and prioritize your pastor's time to be the spiritual leader of the Breakthrough Prayer Initiative. Your pastor doesn't need to be the organizer of every prayer activity. But your pastor does always need to use the spiritual authority of the pastoral role to cast vision, lead the way and tell stories of God's breakthroughs that have begun to happen. Sadly, at churches where the pastor abdicates this responsibility and delegates it to others, the Breakthrough Prayer Initiative rolls to a stop. Your pastor is the leader of the spiritual movement of Jesus that has your church's name—and ensuring the church is feasting on prayer is top priority.

And last, an important Never.

When is it time to cease a Breakthrough Prayer Initiative? When is it over? Never!

Beware. Just as soon as your God-inspired breakthroughs cause you to become busy and distracted with a building project, a church crisis or even a new exciting step forward into which the church is living, it's tempting to let up on leading and fueling your churchwide breakthrough prayer practices you've woven throughout church life. Your time switches to focus instead on tasks and outplay. It's a shift from movement leadership back to management behavior.

And when the church stops praying, asking for new discernment and direction as we surrender our own opinions and desires in order to follow Christ on our greatest expedition, it begins to sit back and become complacent, even indifferent. Plateau can set in, then decline. Members become comfortable enjoying church life for themselves, only offering prayers for those in need or crisis. The church has begun to "snack" on prayer, rather than "feast" on prayer. And if this happens, the body of Christ, the Church, has relinquished its mission-critical nourishment for vitality and movement. It no longer hears the Spirit's call to the open road adventure.

Breakthrough Prayer Initiative

a guide to help you with implementation

1. What ideas, examples and possibilities did you learn about (or think of) as you read *Open Road* chapter 3 that have excited you to consider for your congregation regarding breakthrough prayer? Quickly name these ideas together with your leadership team and write them down here to keep in mind.

2. Now make a list of what *already exists* at your church relative to prayer (meetings that include prayer, worship service prayer, prayer chains, etc.), and how you believe you could add, enhance, renew and/or advance the practice of breakthrough prayer in each setting. What could be done, and how? Be specific.

3. Is there anything at your church currently, related to prayer, that you believe should be discontinued or reinvented? If so, what and when?

4. Look back at the ideas you named together in question #1. What new and unique breakthrough prayer practices could be specifically incorporated into the life of your congregation? In worship, meetings, at other times and settings?

5. How could answers to prayer (breakthroughs, etc.) be regularly reported and celebrated in every setting of the life of your church? Brainstorm what would be most effective, in order to encourage the congregation to recognize and share reports of God's faithfulness and breakthroughs in response to prayer.

6. Think carefully through the next nine months. Then, discuss and plan a timeline for this time period for a Breakthrough Prayer Initiative for your congregation, including the creating and introduction of a short additive congregational breakthrough prayer, adding breakthrough prayer to worship, meetings and all other gatherings, celebrating answers to prayer, incorporating prayer as an integral part of every event or activity, teaching or offering personal breakthrough prayer practices for daily living, etc. as appropriate. Flesh out your specific thoughts below, including potential dates and mile markers for possible implementation.

   What **will be your first next Breakthrough Prayer Initiative "action step" after this discussion?** Let your "start date" be right away!

7. Now close by praying together. Ask God to guide, enhance and bless your vision, the responsiveness of your hearts, the joy and peace of mind and the ongoing outplay of your Breakthrough Prayer Initiative—in order to set the stage for your congregation to head out to the open road of great expedition, expecting God to do beyond what you could ever ask, think or imagine for Christ's Kingdom work!

CHAPTER FOUR

Open Road Survival Equipment:
Specialty Breakthrough Prayer Practices

"Lord, where are you going?" Jesus' traveling companions asked him.

They asked about the intended destination after they had journeyed together following him day after day, mile after mile for what had become years. After they had faced danger, struggle, crowds and challenges together. After they had learned to pray like Jesus, and underway had been transformed into courageous adventurers with risk-taking faith in God's miraculous provision they had seen unfold.

And now near the end of Jesus' earthly life, it was Thomas who asked once again specifically about the journey's destination Jesus had in mind back when he invited each of them to come along. "Lord, we don't know where you are going. So how can we know the way?"

And Jesus explained as simply as he could: "I am

the way, the truth, and the life..." (John 14:5-6).

I wonder whether this news was a surprise to the disciples. After all, typically a journey is supposed to have a specific destination *place* you're trying to reach, right?

Jesus revealed something very different in that moment. He was clarifying that their trek together hadn't merely been a means to arrive at a certain physical destination at all. Rather, Jesus revealed that following him together on the uncharted open road is *itself* the destination—a spiritual one. We, his Church, are intended for perpetual movement. It's the ideal environment for each of us to mature in our faith, deepen our trust, and heed God's distinctive call to bless others with our unique gifts of service. And the most crucial survival equipment to pack along on this greatest expedition are our tools of prayer.

If you've been implementing what you've learned all the way along through these pages, by now your leadership team and congregation have launched a Breakthrough Prayer Initiative that's starting to ripple across the church family. You've become encouraged and hopeful as your leadership team's approach continues to shift, asking God for the

Almighty's supernatural inspiration and discernment regarding what's next for your congregation rather than exclusively strategizing everything yourselves. You are appreciating more and more the dynamics of a "movement" mindset. Moving forward and following Jesus is where you've always wanted to be, and now you and your church have stepped out into the invigorating fresh air of Holy Spirit possibility.

The miraculous ingredient of your church's breakthrough prayer, ongoing, will become a "north star" to keep you expectantly focused up and out, reliant upon the Divine discernment you'll receive to keep advancing. But what about the unexpected, unanticipated, unimagined, untraversed new junctures of the open road that lie up ahead? Might there be occasions when more specialized break-through prayer practices become useful?

Next comes a final recommendation of one more way to keep fueling and renewing your overall Breakthrough Prayer Initiative.

You can further prepare yourselves for movement mindset leadership by creating additional short, specific breakthrough prayer practices that are scripturally based. You'll then have them ready for use if on the open road you encounter adverse conditions such as obstacles, confusing crossroads, or extra-long stretches of travel between fuel stations.

I'd like to help you understand what I mean by providing two examples of specialized breakthrough prayers and their use.

Specific Breakthrough Prayer Practice #1: Mountains into Highways.

> *I will make all My mountains a road,*
> *And My highways will be raised up.*
>
> **Isaiah 49:11 (NASB)**

Have you ever heard of the tiny deep-water port village of Whittier, Alaska? If you intend to drive there from Anchorage, you'll soon be faced with Maynard Mountain towering squarely in the way. How in the world do you get past the mountain blockade? Amazingly, a 2.5 mile long single-lane highway has been cut directly through it. Without the highway right through the mountain, passage would be impossible.

On the open road following Jesus, you may sometimes come upon unexpected vistas when it appears that a "mountain" blocks your way, barring you from going where you believe God is leading. You feel frustration, perhaps anger. Helplessness. A sense of futility. Your mind is racing. Your traveling companions are brainstorming. What to do, what to do, what to do? Is there anything, any way at all we can find to navigate forward? Churches who say yes to the open road adventure understand how this type of dilemma can arise.

Just such a conundrum had settled upon Birch Street Church. Only eighteen months earlier, the leadership team had committed themselves to praying a breakthrough prayer together each day, and had then introduced it to the membership soon after. Pastor Tevin made certain to explain every week during worship that the additional prayer component was to invite God to miraculously reveal the church's next steps. He always emphasized that in order to make room for God's new directional breakthroughs, the church must be willing to surrender its tight, longtime grip on how things had always been done in exchange. Only then would it be possible to receive and discern the Almighty's voice.

The Breakthrough Prayer Initiative had gradually taken hold. Every church committee prayed it at meetings, and began watching and celebrating new breakthroughs of all sizes cropping up in their shared ministry and service. One of those came via a new passion lit inside four members, who began to dream about befriending and serving the students and families of the elementary school right next door. After all, wouldn't that be a route to reaching the next generation—an age group painfully absent in the church's pews?

In anticipation of potential future new younger visitors, the congregation's breakthrough prayer of surrender endowed them with a brand-new willingness to finally sort through and dispose of the contents of closets and multiple unused classrooms that were filled with old church school supplies, drama ministry props from years past, and other unsightly clutter. Volunteers gave hallways and restrooms inexpensive fresh coats of paint. Others invested their gardening skills to enhance the building's curb appeal by overdue shrubbery trimming, cheery flowers and regular lawn care. A spirit of optimism and expectancy pervaded Birch Street Church. God was clearly leading them to prepare for something.

Except...the leadership team that had itself begun the first wave of the breakthrough prayer

was in a conundrum. Due to a '
deaths – most long-time mem'
staunch generous givers to '
minimal financial maintena.
church budget would become impo.
six months. It seemed spiritually parado.
small new ministry effort just starting with th.
school next door, the congregation's new spiritual
nimbleness to actively prepare for new visitors
by readying their building (a project long on the
unfinished strategic planning to-list of the leadership team itself, but now spontaneously motivated
in church members by the Almighty's bidding).
What now?

It seemed heart-breaking to the leadership
team. Just as the church through its Breakthrough
Prayer Initiative was clearly awakening and
surrendering its own preferences and creating
room to receive God's, why had the financial
situation become such an impossible obstacle
in the way? Leadership team members met and
hurriedly put together a list of potential limited
options to explore. A financial assistance grant
from the denomination, perhaps? Even though
the church's annual pledge drive had received a

response, should another financial drive
orth again this soon? Their mountain in the
eemed immovable. With this roadblock, Birch
et Church would be forced to close its doors by
he end of the year.

"I don't understand this at all—we are praying for God to bring us breakthroughs," bemoaned Terry, the leadership team chair, "Why isn't God bringing us the resources we need so we can keep going? Our members love this church, and many have grown up here. What a travesty it would be if our dream to reach the next generation never got to happen? Why, it's obvious God is stirring more and more hearts to be hungry to welcome new young people, even to get the place ready for them to be here."

Pastor Tevin looked thoughtful. "I wonder... hmmm. Of course, we have all been ramping up praying our breakthrough prayer around this. But I wonder if in this instance, we should leverage a slightly different breakthrough prayer right out of scripture? Open your Bibles to Isaiah 49:11, and let me show you what I'm thinking. This is what God redemptively promised to his beloved people of Israel, and I believe still represents the Almighty's continued desire to resource God's Church today:

I will make all My mountains a road,
And My highways will be raised up.
Isaiah 49:11 (NASB)

"I looked at the original Hebrew language in which this verse was written and discovered that 'road' was a Hebrew word elsewhere in the Old Testament also translated into English as 'way' or 'path'– a definite route. It's the same Hebrew word that appears in Psalm 37:5, our church's spring discipleship scripture memory verse. And the Hebrew word translated here as 'highways' was actually, back then, the word used to describe wide public roads intended for heavy traffic.

"Friends, it seems to me this is a reminder that our God continues in the miraculous business of turning mountains into highways, of presenting new routes that haven't appeared to us yet. Using scripture to form breakthrough prayers seems powerful. What if we shift our leadership team's specific breakthrough prayer practice, in light of the 'mountain' we face, to something like this?

God of breakthroughs, we ask you now to
turn mountains into highways. Amen.

Let's pray it together as we adjourn."

The following Sunday, Birch Street Church had a long-scheduled guest preacher in its pulpit for the worship service. Kanesha was the pastor of Lifepointe, a new church start-up in a neighboring part of the city. She filled her sermon that morning with vivid descriptions of the young families with children who were already overcrowding the community center they rented for space to meet. Her message was filled with heartwarming stories of God's miraculous provision at each step of the new congregation's growth, including generous financial commitment of supporters. She finished by affirming that Lifepointe's expansion had all been through the power of saturating everything with prayer. Now she and her leaders were trusting God to provide a much bigger space, one that the burgeoning young congregation could finally make their home. A shortage of space was their biggest obstacle.

The leadership team chair Terry was in attendance, silently praying *Mountains into highways, God. Mountains into highways!* over and over as he looked around the sanctuary at the faces of fellow members who also loved their church. He'd been praying that all week since their meeting. What in the world might God have in mind for their mountain? They'd brainstormed everything, to no avail. *Mountains into highways, God. Mountains into highways!*

He felt like his spirit was shouting the prayer heavenwards.

Then the enthusiastic voice of Pastor Kanesha's preaching garnered his attention. As he listened to the stories of the next-generation-filled Lifepointe Church and heard about their urgent need for more space and classrooms, suddenly he thought of the now-emptied out, cleaned-up unused classrooms right there at Birch Street Church. His eyes suddenly noticed their sanctuary had an abundance of empty seating.

What in heaven's name? he wondered. *Is our highway through this mountain a merger with Lifepointe Church? Is God's way to accomplish our dream to reach the next generation by surrendering our own church's identity and building to form a new one together?* His heart pounded. This idea was completely crazy. Birch Street Church members had always loved their own traditions and ways of doing things, their own rules and policies. Would they be willing to consider surrendering everything as they had always known it, in order to merge with the young Lifepointe Church as a next step to their dream? Why, this could be a potential God-breakthrough of unprecedented proportion.

After the worship service, Terry hurried to catch Pastor Kanesha and asked for a moment of her time. He also pulled in Pastor Tevin, and together the three found a corner of the entryway to talk. His breakthrough idea came spilling out, words tumbling over each other, as he spoke aloud the possibility that had come to him during the sermon. He concluded by telling Pastor Kanesha about the church's Breakthrough Prayer Initiative, and the specific *Mountains into highways* prayer practice the leadership team had so recently deployed. Could this possibly be the breakthrough that both Lifepointe and Birch Street Church had been praying for?

The previous months the congregation had invested in their Breakthrough Prayer Initiative seemed to have an impact. When a members meeting was called to introduce and explore the merger opportunity, Birch Street Church's growing spiritual nimbleness, learning to surrender personal preferences in order to make room for God's breakthroughs, was evident. Vigorous, healthy discussion took place. Honest grief was expressed as they heard about potential necessary changes to how their church had always operated, should the merger be affirmed. But they voted to wholeheartedly explore the merger idea.

Both congregations joined together in the *Mountains into highways* breakthrough prayer practice, gathering jointly to pray and walk through Birch Street's building more than once. And Birch Street Church hosted a summer picnic and games party on its large back lawn, inviting Lifepointe's many families and children to worship and begin new friendships together.

Later when each congregation voted on the merger, their collective decision was a green light. And when the Lifepointe and Birch Street leadership teams met to begin crafting first steps together as one church, Terry realized he felt the irresistible breeze of open road movement resuming in his heart once more. A word rose heavenward from his spirit:

> *Thank you, Jesus, and wherever you take us next on this spiritual expedition, you've shown all of us that always, our prayer practices make all the difference....*

Breakthrough Prayer Practice #2: Grant Us Peace.

Now may the Lord of peace Himself continually grant you peace in every circumstance.

2 Thessalonians 3:16 NASB

An anonymous fable recounts the story of an old farmer who had worked lifelong in his fields. One day his horse escaped and vanished. When the neighbors heard, they came by to see him. "Oh, my—such bad luck!" they sympathized. "Maybe," the farmer answered.

The next day his horse returned to the farm, bringing along three other wild horses. "How wonderful!" the neighbors celebrated. "Maybe," the farmer answered.

The following day, the farmer's son tried to train one of the new wild horses. He was thrown off, and broke his leg. Again, the neighbors tried to console him, saying, "What misfortune!" "Maybe," the farmer replied.

The day after that, military officials came to town to draft young men for the army. Since the son's leg was broken, they passed him by. The neighbors congratulated the farmer on how things turned out. "Maybe," said the farmer.

Oh, the tension, the paradox illuminated by this fable! It's the same paradox you'll discover out on the open road together following Jesus. As your church, now a movement fueled by prayer for new possibilities, moves onward with its next spiritual expedition, you'll also experience the tension of the "maybe."

Is the change and impact of our new directional discernment going to be joyful or difficult for us? Maybe.

Will it stretch us, or will it unite us? Maybe.

Will our own ideas of what should happen get to take place, or will strange and unfamiliar outplays replace them? Maybe.

Will everyone stay with us as we journey, or will some choose not to go further and newcomers come along instead? Maybe.

In the midst of the ambiguity and tension that's inherent in group open road travel on an unknown path following a purposeful leader named Jesus, it becomes more important than ever to listen closely to Divine directions.

Remember back to chapter 2's story about my meeting with Faith Church's leadership team at their future focus session? Afterwards, Pastor Milton kept in contact. He let me know the good news that not only had the team adhered to their "What if..." prayer covenant, they had also pushed their Breakthrough Prayer Initiative churchwide. Members had been adding the short breakthrough prayer to their daily lives. And as they set aside their own preferences, God had room within some to stir fresh ideas and desires of entirely new ministry service possibilities for which they now felt passion.

Then one day, Pastor Milton emailed to ask if I could join his leadership team at their next meeting. He wrote that there was frustration afoot between some of them, and others were convinced nothing seemed to be happening even with all the prayer.

At the meeting they quickly brought me up to date. All the breakthrough prayer had indeed ignited new ministry interests in many across the congregation. Excitement was high. The leadership team had organized those with new ideas to be investigated into research task forces. Each task force was given six weeks to gather more information, investigate potential, continue praying the breakthrough prayer together, prayer walk whatever settings the new ministry ideas might take

place, and receive God's discernment how and w.
any of the new possibilities might be part of God's
new direction for Faith Church.

It was now only the third week, and thus far the
leadership team had heard nothing back early from
any of the task forces.

Remember Jeffrey? You won't be surprised
that he was the first to jump impatiently into the
discussion. "Listen. I already told you, last time
you were with us, that reciting prayers all the time
is not what I signed up for when I agreed to serve
on the leadership team. I thought we were finally
moving forward, but now we seem just to be waiting
around, losing time and doing nothing much other
than praying while the new research task forces
are doing whatever they are doing. It's stressful! My
only real goal is to try to help the church organize
to do something worthwhile for our community. But
we're letting church members do the research on
what they're passionate about, instead of us leaders
who know better?"

Disagreement broke out, as a few team members
defended the creation of the member-led research
task force groups. Jeffrey continued anyway.

"Bottom line, this church feels like a car that's

ne moment. So, with all due respect to

ayer which we've already now tried,

to what we still want to find out: Pastor

able to help us or not with a practical plan that will get our motor going, pulled out of the garage and finally moving?"

All eyes turned to me for a response.

"You've set me up perfectly with your metaphor of a car that won't start, for a related metaphor I'd hoped to use. Thank you for that segue, Jeffrey. Maybe this will help." Out of my work bag I pulled out an old, well-used paper road map that I unfolded and placed it so all could see.

"Why, maps like those used to be a dime a dozen at any gas station," Ben exclaimed. "In fact, my wife and I still refer to those as gas station maps. Back in the day, that's all we had if we needed to go someplace we'd never gone before. Beforehand we would study the map and use a red marker to draw a line along our route. Then I would drive, and she as the passenger would have the map open on her lap, trying to follow along our red line and tell me when and where to turn."

"How did that work for you?" I asked.

"Sometimes okay, but usually not well," Ben

laughed. "My wife had a habit of noticing too late that I needed to turn, so I would miss it and have to circle back. Back then the gas station maps were also always outdated, so it was typical for us to discover that there were new streets not on the map, or there always seemed to be road construction going on with sudden detours. Nowadays, I wouldn't even consider using a gas station paper map."

"What do you use now?" I asked.

"Well, thank goodness for modern-day GPS, of course! Honestly, I don't even try to figure out a route to someplace new ahead of time now. I just listen and follow the GPS voice coming from my phone real-time as I drive. And unless I quit listening because I'm talking to my wife and not paying attention, the GPS voice does a pretty darn good job of giving me timely heads-up so I know where to turn, when to avoid road construction and even what to watch out for. I only have to stay attentive, look and listen, that's all, to get where we hope to go. In fact, I just told someone the other day that now I don't like to drive anyplace new, even shorter distances, without the GPS turn by turn directions speaking to me. Can't imagine trying to get there using one of those old paper maps now like you've got."

I pulled out hard copies of the last three years of the church's future focus plans that Pastor Milton had sent me. "Hmmm. Do you suppose that each of these future focus outlines of plans for where you wanted to go in each upcoming year, the ones you have been creating and recreating annually in the past, are a little like attempting to use a gas station map?"

"What in the world do you mean?" Jeffrey asked defensively. "How else would we find our way forward, without outlining an airtight strategy plan to work from like we always do?"

"I'm all for the idea of naming potential ways to progress," I assured him. "The catch is, however, that when we only brainstorm and create our own routes to get there according to what we think might be possible from our limited human perspective, experience and practical common sense, it's just that: our collective, informed opinion about what we would like to have happen, what ought or logically should happen next. It's a common approach. But that's not who you are. You here are leaders of the miraculous, living movement of Jesus called the Church—something distinctly different."

"Ah, maybe I get it!" The light was dawning for

gas-station-map Ben. "Are you suggesting that when the church behaves like a movement—becomes a group of people following Jesus and praying for breakthroughs and open-door guidance to God's new possibilities—our ongoing prayers allow the Holy Spirit to provide us real-time turn-by-turn guidance and discernment as we move forward? That is, if we're not just busy talking to each other or arguing about our own route ideas, and are paying attention and listening? Is that the analogy? Wow. If that's what you're saying, that's a big reason to let the research task forces continue their investigation and prayer discernment. We just need to stay the course in the meantime."

Chairperson Claire then spoke up slowly. "I believe with all my heart that it was God's direction—our leadership team's discernment—to create and empower the research task forces among our membership as they explore their new ministry passions. And we did set six full weeks as their time frame.

"As we talk about driving and listening carefully to GPS turn by turn guidance, I'm suddenly remembering what it's always like when I drive west from here for nearly four hours to go visit our relatives. The GPS voice is guiding me frequently as I navigate my way out of our city and get on to the interstate. But then the GPS voice is literally silent for hours as I continue on the interstate across the state. I used to find myself checking during the drive to make sure I was still supposed to just stay the course, since the GPS guidance wasn't speaking. But now I've learned that if I do accidentally turn off, the GPS will guide me back. So, I don't worry about it anymore, and try to enjoy the long peaceful drive for what it is. I've left where I started, but am not yet where I'm going and I won't be for a while.

"I believe we likewise need to be patient and stay our course right now and keep praying for our research task forces' work. We haven't stalled out; we are simply underway."

"Right there is our point of tension," Jeffrey said. "Sure, God might intend us to stay the course while the task forces are working. But what if they come up empty-handed, and we will have lost six precious weeks we could have been using to figure out something ourselves? What if we're forced to scramble? Or at the other extreme, what if they come back with proposals that are unprecedented in scope and impact at a level we've never dealt with before?"

"I am so encouraged with your commitment to the Faith Church breakthrough prayer, and how you continue to train the entire congregation, all ages, to add it to their prayer lives regularly," I said. "Now, I'd like to introduce to you a specialty breakthrough prayer practice to consider using in this season of 'Maybe.' That's what season you're in, isn't it? Maybe the task forces will deliver potential-packed new directions. Maybe they won't. Maybe the new open road following Jesus on which you find yourselves will bring a new turn. Maybe is everywhere around. I've come to realize that the great expedition on which we all find ourselves trains us to become 'People of the Maybe.' It's the attitude required of us to be led on a spiritual journey.

"This is a short specialty breakthrough prayer practice especially useful in 'Maybe' seasons like yours. It's based on 2 Thessalonians 3:16:

Now may the Lord of peace Himself continually grant you peace in every circumstance.

"The original Greek word for 'peace' used here literally means tranquility. Quietness in spirit. Harmony with others. And the Greek word we've translated 'continually grant' is an expansive one, extending and bestowing more and more upon us. Interestingly, 'circumstance' is a Greek world depicting character, our personal deportment behavior. It seems we are to understand that Jesus, our Lord of peace, intends to break through abundantly in us with his brand of peace. It will evidence itself not only by our calm demeanors even when we're in a season of waiting to see what's next, and also in how we treat others while we wait.

"The breakthrough prayer practice that seems to emerge from this scripture is *Grant us peace.* Christ's peace, as people living in the tension of the Maybe. Could this be your next breakthrough prayer to incorporate as a leadership team? *Grant us peace.*"

Pastor Milton smiled. "That's a good next breakthrough prayer for us. Let's adopt it right now! What a reminder that there's a vast difference between resignation and surrender. Jeffrey, it's not that we resign ourselves to wait for the research task forces to complete their work. We surrender our own preferences in order to live into the timing of our road trip leader, Jesus. Do we trust his timing more than we trust our human sense of timing? I read someplace this week that complaining is a symptom of the internal battle of spiritual surrender. And that blame will also always block faith. Everyone, let's do our best to keep looking up and out, and pray our way into becoming peace-filled people of the Maybe. I like the sound of that, do you?"

Today I keep framed on my desk a card that I received from Jeffrey about six months after the second meeting with Faith Church's leadership team. Inside he had written an update of celebration about the exciting steps that were finally unfolding there.

The quote stamped on the front of the card continues to challenge me, on my own spiritual journey, to live as a Person of the Maybe:

> *Deciding everything is falling into place*
> *perfectly, as long as you don't get too picky about*
> *what you mean by place. Or perfectly.*
>
> **Brian Andreas**

And finally—Godspeed for what's ahead!

As you and I part ways now, may you be encouraged by holy expectation as you actively affirm with your lives that prayer indeed makes all the difference.

Let's stay in touch! You can reach me anytime to share your own breakthroughs and new breakthrough prayer practices, plus find other churches' breakthrough prayer video stories, interviews, resources and new prayer learnings, at **snkibbey.com**.

Now may the God of hope fill you with all joy and peace in believing, so that you will abound in hope by the power of the Holy Spirit.

Romans 15:13 NASB

Made in USA - Kendallville, IN
80090_9781950899210
08.30.2023 1340